TURNS AND RETURNS

Poems and Paintings
by
George Hitchcock

Library of Congress Control Number 2002100635
ISBN 0-9679315-4-1

Philos Press
524 Palm Street
Santa Rosa, CA 95404

For Marjorie

Thanks to the editors of *Caliban, Durak, Moons & Lions, Monk's Pond, StarDancer, The New Student Review, Cloud Marauder, Changes, Three Rivers, Burning Water, The San Marcos Review, Beatitude, Midwest,* and *Bird Effort,* where versions of these poems first appeared.

Portions of the interview with George Hitchcock appeared in *Durak,* No. 1, 1978.

Selections from *The Piano Beneath the Skin,* © 1978 by George Hitchcock, are reprinted with the permission of Copper Canyon Press, P.O. Box 271, Port Townsend, WA 98368-0271.

Photo of George Hitchcock courtesy of Marjorie Simon.

Oil pastels by George Hitchcock are reproduced on pages 9, 23, 41, 53, 71 and 85.

The cover painting: La Biciclista, 1999.

CONTENTS

INTRODUCTION

In 1969 Beau Beausoleil and I came to San Francisco to be where poetry was happening. We brought with us $100, two suitcases, sturdy shoes to walk the city's hills, and a burning itch to read, hear, and write poetry. We also carried a riffled copy of *Kayak*. Beau had discovered surrealism in its pages and liked it. I would soon like it too, discovering for the first time strange and wonderful ways to use language.

We found an apartment to house our suitcases and soon set out like pilgrims to visit George Hitchcock, *Kayak's* editor. Beau wanted to be published in *Kayak* in the worst way. With our new shoes, but no map, we walked twenty-eight blocks from Haight Street up Laguna Street, hill after hill, until we found the house.

This first conversation was not awkward, considering we were two total strangers showing up on his doorstep on a Saturday morning. We were especially excited when George invited us to attend the next weekend the moveable feast that was "kayaking." Whenever George had finished hand printing a new issue of the magazine, his basement overflowed with an eclectic group of people all associated with *Kayak* in some way, friends, associates, artists, and poets and writers both on and off the prominence meter. In the middle of the room people gathered around a huge table, hand collating from individual towers of paper, while on side tables others put the cover on, stapled, trimmed books. There were sandwiches and beer for lunch, and spirited encounters around the table's periphery. In this conviviality, a whole generation kayaked, including Raymond Carver, James Houston, Peter Beagle, Robert Peterson, Adam Cornford, Lennart Bruce, Larry Fixel, Clem Starck, Nanos Valaoritis, among many others. And then when George moved to Santa Cruz, since we didn't have a car we kayaked less frequently, but we did our best to find a ride to what was always wonderful fun.

I wanted to be in *Kayak* too, but it was to be my collages that George published. He answered his mail quickly and we knew that soon, too soon, after the poems were sent out that judgment would follow. We received interesting rejections, brief and pointed, the most memorable, and confusing, being to Beau. It stated with an exclamation mark that he had written "the penultimate poem." We looked up penultimate in the dictionary, and shrugged.

A Ship of Bells was the first book of George's I read and those poems resonate upon re-reading, alive with musicality, words sensuous as a lover's, and magical in their imagery, as do all the poems I have discovered and re-discovered in the selection process for this book.

My sole criteria in appreciating any literary or visual art work is whether it moves me or not. "Pick what you like, as I would," George said when asked what poems to include here, and I have. Like a child, scattering around bits of shiny paper, only to find when reassembling them, that they are stars.

—Laura Beausoleil, Publisher

The Poet, 2000

1.

"Poetry, to me, is accompanied by a release of the imagination which I can accomplish by the methods of Surrealism. Thus far I am a Surrealist. No further.

The process of creation is mystical, but I don't put mystical names on it. (To begin a poem) I put myself in a position where I can be dictated to. What comes out, I write down. But what I write down, I don't treat as a sanctified text. I fiddle with it, rewrite it and try to find the center of it. In poetry, I always start with the idea of music. I enjoy writing poetry; when the day comes that I don't enjoy writing poetry, I'll stop it. The real task of my poetry is to discover the extent and geography of my own subconscious. And then put that down in the most intelligible fashion reconcilable with the subconscious. And I utilize all the words I know to do it."

— from interview with George Hitchcock
in *Durak,* No. 1

CONSIDER THE POET

who walks in a stony field behind his plow
turning up old flints
adze-heads and the bones of ptarmigan,
. who lives in terror of tea-leaves
ink-blots and mendicant feathers,
who spends his tears on jujubes
and on feastdays
pulls coins from dirty ears
to the applause of grassblades;

whose overcoat is specked with the dandruff
of alphabets; a salamander
born in the hospitable lava, he
traffics in scoriac mysteries
and scalds the hands of those
who put trust in him:

arbiter of waters, nuncio of the wild iris,
Ishmaelite among the tenements of eyes,
you salute each morning the flags
which flutter in the cottonwoods
and bear in your lung the deadly flower
of recollection.

KEEP CLOSE TO AVOID THE WEIR

The river ingests the reeds
the swans lead the small boats
of their young
in search of glass confections

There are cyclists on the towpath
women leaning from the stone arches
the flags of new wash
whip in the June wind

Overhead the swallows
cast their purposeful nets,
in the earth underfoot the cities
of ants prosper and fall

— And yet my own life here
at Iffley near Oxford a coil
of rope a bleached board
a hawser aimlessly
basking by the locks

—

Out of profound
dissatisfaction
I make this song.

VARIATIONS ON THREE POEMS BY HEINE

1.

Yesterday you danced for me,
thoughtless of all recompense
and in movement's ecstasy
whirled in the wind
a poplar
a froth
a golden bird.

Today I would have you dance again
and Herod shall not outdo me:
turn, golden bird,
poplar in the wind,
turn!
And, executioner,
at the south gate you'll find the Baptist:
decapitate him.

2.

By the loud sweep and harsh unending roll
of surf on sand, how bitterly
you watch the sun drop
into the sea.
But I,
who know its conjurer's tricks
and how you're half in love with doom,
begrudge it not its brief nap
in that wet room

but think rather as in front of us
it plunges bankrupt in the sea
how soon behind us it will rise
triumphantly.

3.

If I with roses in your praise
fill these streets and these rooms
remember
underneath the metaphors

a fire runs and coals burn
secretly.

And should among those wax bouquets
a spark or two appear —
do not fear —
for the world believes not in flames
and will consider them
mere poetry.

STILL LIFE

apples
nectarines
& carafes
gyre in their
waxed re
flection the
sun flies
through the
window &
sheds
its feathers
over the wine glass
a fork
dozes in
the rumpled
napkin
a lion leaps
from the
zinnias
runs down
mahogany
biceps & dis
appears into
a woven
aztec
jungle

FANTASY ON EIGHT PAINTINGS
BY S. ROSOVSKY

1.

the red face of ruin a mirror in her hand
omphalos of creased skin fleshy spirals
under the outstretched arms of umbrellas

2.

tortured figures gather in a room
of bent doors wine-colored tiles and four
bearded patients who wait for the one
who never comes old bonecrusher
blue memory his whiskers frozen stiff

3.

a dog immense as a bumblebee dazzles
the daisies while compact in their igloo
sit Goodman Shem and his naughty children

4.

roses in the linoleum versatile
at the pianola their monstrous child
tinkling the keys of grief while in urban
hells his naked progenitors grapple and smirk

5.

the moulding is loose and bluebottle flies
creep from the tattered wainscoting

6.

a cherub with a tin whistle feeds
the doves holding its wrist out to
a mother's mirror which
shows a broken toy where once were eyes

7.

on the mansard consumptive uncles with
wayward flutes and along the nave
arm chairs grow like cancer the long aisles
yellow with hopelessness

8.

the city falls
to an onslaught of fungus in the flooded
plaza an armless man writhes
his belly covered with termites

THE HERRING RUN

Morning after morning I awake
to find some lines formed in sleep
waiting for the morning's light
to give them shape and lineament

but nothing that I've done
takes its hoped-for form
because for a week now the herring have run
and distracted I walk on the pier
to watch those spawning nations
silver the sea with their desire;
while swirling in the sky above
terns, gulls and cormorants
rend and devour
what the blind love of fishes brings.

morning after morning I awake
to that tide of love, those raucous wings
and every sober thought of sober things
becomes somehow and against my will decoyed
by those caws and flutterings —

till angry with myself I must write down
this epitaph for high thoughts destroyed
by the clatter of wings.

AFTERNOON IN THE CANYON

The river sings in its alcoves of stone.
I cross its milky water on an old log —
beneath me waterskaters
dance in the mesh of roots.
Tatters of spume cling
to the bare twigs of willows.

The wind goes down.
Bluejays scream in the pines.
The drunken sun enters a dark mountainside,
its hair full of butterflies.
Old men gutting trout
huddle about a smoky fire.

I must fill my pockets with bright stones.

WEDNESDAY MATINEE

I leave the per
verse canyons of
motors the scarves
of fog and the tired
vows of newsprint.

A woman with eyes
of brocade marks
my ticket with her
lipstick I am
surrounded by oct
agonal desires and
effusive corsets.

Suburban ankles
rise like stanchions
around me there is
the sudden lilt of
silk violas the
lights go down.

On the screen some
metaphors with
moustaches act
out my secret
life as acro
bat and spy.

THE ROMANTIC

Following a secret
star no bigger
than a snowflake

his hat tied to a
kite of pain he
limps (nose fore

most) out of the
glacier. Dressed
in an old horse

blanket medallions
on his heart and
beard burred

he walks among the
stray cows. Looking
for something braided

a knotted sheet a
ladder anything
to lead him out

of this century.

Plowing, 2000

2.

 I start writing and I never look at a word the moment I put it down. That's the only way you can induce and maintain that state of consciousness. If you stop and look, you're lost. The idea in this sort of writing — automatic writing — is to free yourself from all grammatical and critical worries. Just start writing and allow one word to discover the next word without thinking about it. Pretty soon one word leads to another. If you get expert at releasing your subconscious and releasing your sense of play or accident, it goes pretty well. When you go back and read it, every word is a surprise.

— from interview with George Hitchcock
  in *Durak*, No. 1

LYING NOW IN THE NEW GRASS

the wind falls the fields
fold in upon each other
like wings on a sleeping
insect. The house heavy
with the day's sweat sighs
beneath the hand of dusk.

All things sleep:
lilac iris bracken
windmill & anvil
the stones which dream
of moss the cold stars
in endless heaven.

Now may all rutting lovers
under this lace of leaves
lie down in comfort.
Let them not hear the dew form
over the pastures nor foresee
its sharp hooves in the loam.
May the plow of night
pass over them.

EARLY JUNE ON RAFFERTY CREEK

The trail enters an alpine
meadow banners of sedge
            flap at my knees
            underfoot
the resilience of the breathing
            turf:
            gray eyes
on the willow twigs.

The ice embarks on its final
            pilgrimage,
            bridges
with melting feet collapse
            into the creek;
            in the choke-
cherry thicket a brown towhee
            scratches
            for worms
beneath the dying snow.

I blow on my chilled hands —
see how breath burns
            in the green wind!

NOVEMBER

The earth frozen
leaves ascend ladders
of smoke   sky
whispers with twigs.

The blackberry bush
is bare a skater
spins on the stubborn ice;

thorns; thorns;

I must mend the flue
before winter creeps out
like an earwig.

DAWN

Clouds rise from their nests
with flapping wings, they whisper
of worn leather, bracken, long
horizons, and the manes of dark
horses. In the waking stream
the stones lie like chestnuts
in a glass bowl. I pass the bones
of an old harrow thrown on its side
in the ditch.

                Now the sun appears.
It is a fish wrapped in straw.
Its scales fall on the sleeping
town with its eyeless granaries
and necklace of boxcars. Soon
the blue wind will flatten the roads
with a metallic palm, the glitter
of granite will blind the eyes.

But not yet. The beetle still
stares from the riding moon, the ship
of death stands motionless on
frozen waves: I hear
the silence of early morning
rise from the rocks.

THE SWIM

Gravel
a broken seawall
the red buoy
barnacles adrift
on a thatch
of water Dredges
piers & pilings
arthritic with shells
the odor of oil
varnished waves
with fingers of
kelp Caws Cries
& Silence &
over all the
glittering shell
of heaven

A whiskered
seal rises
beside me
like a drowned
prophet

THE REHEARSAL

Under the frost, new grass;
in the sky small clouds
round as daisies. Spring
unfolds: inside her soft corolla
bees hum. The sky,
stiff as iron, supports
the gold wings of finches.

I walk past the rotting ciderpress.
Grouse explode in the air about me.
The voice of the wind issues
from a wooden throat
with its old moanings
and hairy pressures.

Now it will all begin again.

THE ASCENSION

Flotillas of leaves set sail in the birch trees.
They are answering the call of birds, their brothers;
they too would like to ascend like sonatas of glass
from pianos, but the twigs, the limbs, the roots
hold them back.

                    In such an April
we would all fly upward like sparks, but some emblem
in our shoes detains us.

FIELDS NEAR PENDLETON

their crests of wild flax
their troughs filled with shadow
the long groundswells the wind makes
under a froth of grain.

A combine comes over the horizon
full-rigged, leaning into a gale of chaff.
A flock of pilgrim geese undulates
in the cloudless sky.

Waiting for some message I sit
in the shade of an old oak
but the birds have gone
and I hear the creaking only
of that ghostly immense ship
which harvests the waves.

THE GIFT

Catkins fallen from the alders
float on the water's surface.

The bicycles are leaner. Under the foot-
bridge there are new fronds of fern.

The faces of unknown poets drift
in the sky disguised as plumes of mist.

Spring enters my window
carrying a small bouquet of steeples.

A HOT DAY WITH LITTLE RESULT

The fish have grown torpid.
They avoid me.
I rest in the shade of a covered bridge —
its planks thunder beneath the logging trucks.

The stream breathes softly
in the roots of cottonwoods,
it sends out secret messages of dust
to the suave rushes.

A farmer on a red tractor
spreads corduroy on the hill opposite me.
The meadow-rue is in bloom.
There is no use fishing.

I sit in the shade and think
of that great tortoise who carries
the Bay of Naples on his back.

ALARM

Fire! fire! I hear
at the edge of my dream.
The horses whinny.
The dry ferns curl into flame.
The animals paw the earth.
I run.

Yes, always I run:
backwards through old fevers
leaving these heavy years
and meaningless bridges.
Vaulting the stile
I shout, fire! fire!
in the field of the red bull.

PASTORALE

By the brick groves
at the pier-end
children stand on the green
banks of slime fauns
with bottlecaps on
their throats their hair
sparkling with gems
of junk metal torn
from the flanges
of the sun;

the sea stretches
its green muscles
over the tideflats the
cranes turn
into their dark houses
night comes.

Near the sub-
way's mouth a rose
of newsprint blossoms
on the shoulder
of a dreaming kiosk.

THE SCAFFOLDINGS I WEAR

old coats of habit, off
with them! their stanzas
of coal-tar, their endless
hexameters of gasoline!

I'll telephone the tailors
of charred cork and drift-
wood, the maskers of winds,
the thimbles blazing

in the seams of mullein,
the scissors which open
on harbors of flags,
on Sundays gnawed

by tempest and on those old
piers whose eyelashes
are stitched with spume.
And if it's not too late

I'll write down
the haberdashery
of small birds
garbed in mist,

of semaphores hidden
in clouds, of the canals
which lose themselves
in mouths of grass,

and the naked raindrops
which like parachutists
hang
from the homes of spiders.

THE MOUNTAINS

the mountains gallop through the sky
their manes combed their saddle-cinches
tightened the mountains have nostrils
of ice and their eyes are glacial lakes
high in the moraine

they're bridled by wanderers with secret
violins in their saddlebags dreamers
who thirst for the nectar of stones
pilgrims who ask forgiveness
of their basalt teeth
who ask the mountains where
they're going and whether it's true
they're the daughters of midnight

the mountains don't answer
they shake their white heads and paw
the valleys with granite hooves
they've ridden far these mountains
they know a lot they keep threatening
to turn into constellations
and lose themselves in the vast
pastures of the Milky Way

Desire, 1998

3.

" I want to create a sense of wonder and mystery on which the reader can project himself and fantasize. To do that, one must wrench accepted reality. You pull it apart. You throw it a little out of kilter, a little out of gear. This encourages the creative act of reading and the projection of fantasy on the part of the reader.

The poetic experience is like a spark which goes from one pole to another pole—it bridges and leaps. In order to make that flash which is the *frisson* of a poetic experience, there must be not only the mind that creates but there must be the mind that receives it. That mind is the reader's. "

— from interview with George Hitchcock
in *Durak,* No. 1

LYING ON MY BACK LOOKING UPWARD

through the sumac leaves
the air sparkles with motes
and the fleecy pavilions
of flying spiders;

a hundred feet toward heaven
the new fronds of the redwood
are a lighter green in
the dark tracery.

A friend is hurling oak sticks
to an eager black dog
which, given its will, would
devour the forest branch by branch.

What is important is not
to pursue love for it will always
elude you; rather
to make yourself worthy

to receive it should,
like these shimmering webs
in the afternoon sun,
it be silently offered.

RITES OF PASSAGE

I return from errands of penance
I speak with the voice of the cicada
I paint my face with clay and coal

I linger at well's lip drawing
ceaselessly circles in dust
for four days now I've dwelt
in the harsh camp of madness

under the lodgepole roses burn
magic flowers false plumes
the ritual bird which turns and turns
inside its own shadow

rabbitfur snakeskin
teeth of the beaver
dried bundles of alder twigs
where the god has built his altar

the old men speak they offer me
buckskin saddle
a bow of ash a pale horse
and mandalas of sacred smoke

I fall silent
I wrap myself in the nightwind
stars sprout like young barley
in the dark fields

on the fifth day I grow weak with fasting
on the sixth day I hear sledrunners creak in the snow
on the seventh day gates will be thrown back
and I shall speak to the gold snake
coiled in the sun

VOYAGING TO THE ANTIPODES

I embark now from this land
of stone botanies and enter
the sea. I plunge my arm

in her secret places.
My compass turns to ichor.
I sink.

From her lips
there grow savage bouquets
of kelp. Between her hips

the drowned grind
in their dance. I join them.
Cleanse me, woman,

of asphalt, of diffidence,
of the rage of wires!
My bush floats like

a lotus in her green depth.
I uncoil into sleep, her
turbulence subsides.

Day comes, the waves
tread one by one
to customary beaches.

The sun blinks. She
awakes. Her eyes are dry
stones, her spray

my sweat, my kissed mouth
chafed by salt.

Sargassos of what
latitudes?
Under what stars?

PARANOIA

some morning even the rivers
run uphill the wild barley bursts

into flight and black fists
of storm threaten my sanity

I'm called from the room
by a woman whose voice whirrs

like cicadas in a grove of pines
to the place where four vultures

scrabble in cross-roads' dust
their talons and beaks in a bundle

of bloodied rags while overhead
the moon swathed in white writing

whirls through the mist
like a glittering fish-hook

ON THIS FIRST DAY OF APRIL
I STARE IN WONDER

at the fountains and their agile tongues
the buds afloat in the azaleas
the larks in their circus
the eloquent pebbles moaning in the creek

at the yellow breath of the newborn acacia
at the wild mustard sailing toward heaven
the stars which turn cartwheels in the sod

and your wrist sun-ringed now
with a bracelet of grace

AN ILLUMINATION

Alone in the room
its walls hung
with trophies
of gesso & plaster

And then as in smoked
glass you appear
with aureole of flame
& onyx eyes

I hear your laughter
& open my stained
hands to your dress
of tapestry

In the green thighs
of that woven forest a thunder
cloud swells: you fall
backward into
longing

EIDOLON

woman of saffron and lilac
woman of the great mane of moonbeams
woman who sleeps under a canopy
knit with two bronze needles
woman who leads the stars to drink
from Africa and nestles
comets in her soft hand

woman whose banners advance leading
the armies of absence woman
who emits whirlwinds and floats
over our heads in cloud bandages
woman whose bare feet are clipper
ships traversing extinct oceans

woman who bears twelve children
one for each month and suckles the days
woman of the gondola and liquid cavern
woman of flute-flames
of the orchestra of navels
of the scarlet stairway which leads
into the tarn of the guitar

woman of hibiscus
woman of the flamboyant-tree
woman incommensurate whose structure
rises like a conch-shell over the sunrise
woman of feathers and pinnate leaves
of curly wool and eyes disguised
in mothwings woman of flesh
without compasses without numerals
woman of the birth of color
woman of the nude violoncello
and the umbilical cord
tied to the cathedral of snow

THE ACT

Bareback, she balances on a wish
of steam. I hear her magnetic voice,

I see her eyes which are thistles,
the creased poppy of her sex.

Her whip cracks. I sing my campaigns
of grace, my legends of sawdust,

recounting the loves which flew
from cisterns of rust, my meetings

with masks and dragonflies, forays
into those gardens under the sea.

The voice of the phonograph dies
on the dying air. My histories

collapse like fans. I see them now
for what they are — mists, maggots,

odd corners of old trials
that ended in fog. The whip cracks.

The children's hour is over. Again
I'll leap through that paper hoop.

THE ONE WHOSE REPROACH
I CANNOT EVADE

She sits in her glass garden
and awaits the guests —
The sailor with the blue tangerines
the fish clothed in languages
the dolphin with a revolver in its teeth.

Dusk enters from stage left:
its voice falls like dew on the arbor.
Tiny bells
sway in the catalpa tree.

What is it she hopes to catch in her net
of love? Petals? Conch-shells?
The night-moth? She does not speak.
Tonight, I tell her, no one comes;
you wait in vain.

Yet at eight precisely
the moon opens its theatric doors,
an arm rises from the fountain,
the music box, face down
on her tabouret, swells and bursts
its cover — a tinkling flood of
rice moves over the table.

She smiles at me, false believer,
smiles and goes in, leaving
the garden empty and my thighs
half-eaten by the raging twilight.

Weeping Machine, 2001

4.

"A lot of people say I use a lot of long words. If I use a lot of long words, it's because I'm familiar with a lot of long words. They're part of my life. A loving attitude toward words is one thing that a poet must have. The poet cares for words and one word is distinctive, has a wonderful sound, is absolutely irreplaceable. It is the *mot juste*, as Flaubert said, while another word is hackneyed, cliched, overworked. You have to develop that sensitivity to language."

— from interview with George Hitchcock
in *Durak,* No. 1

EVENTS OF OUR EPOCH

oil is discovered in the crowns
    of hats and is piped
    out of melodious stockings
a symphony somewhat wider than
    Australia
    is performed under Niagara
    Falls to the applause
    of anxious cannonballs
the construction of unemployed
    kidneys is voted
    precedence over
    carrousels & parallelepipeds
elegant hydroponic forests
    of chanterelles
    populate the space
    platforms
kerosene lanterns are hastily
    organized into brigades
    for the conquest of
    Mount Situ-Nervosa
male children whose names begin
    with semi-colons are
    granted
    placentas of cocaine
embalmed deodorized dentures
    are worshipped in
    the Cathedral of spasm

Zeus hurls an immense dais
   in the general
   direction
   of the prostate gland
access to electro-shock
   therapy is
   limited to
   those under ninety
Congress passes a law
   forbidding
   epaulets on bicycles
the penalty: amputation
   of one's
   shadow

MOLOCH

the dome of his forehead rises over the pyramids
his tongue lies alone a bone in the desert

his eyelids are painted with gold leaf
his brows lined with henna and kohl

his teeth appear to be stars
his mouth opens to eat clocks

his hands are gloves stuffed with sand
his feet are glued to their own shadows

geysers of locusts spray from his penis
his knees come apart like Chinese puzzles

in the boulevards of his gut
the machinery grinds endlessly

under his palate a concealed phonograph
this message this message this message

is recorded

ARMORED BEAST

he crawls over the flanks
of obsidian peaks

in the northern night he
grumbles among pinons

his snout pressed deep
in wet roots *erethizon*

epixanthum the porcupine
he reads the messages

left by glaciers chews
the resinous pinebark

the shoots of red alder
and hemlock I know

his green search his
spines are inside me

ranged in my gut
like tiers of nails

I am cousin to that hunger
blind in my night as he

SIVA THE DESTROYER

A holy hum rises
from the inward moons
of his vision. He speaks:
there are caves in his teeth.

He climbs the wheel
of the hours;
his torso whirls
in a pagoda of sulphur.

Clockwork arms
grow from his hips.
He sits on the throne
of the frozen yellow sun.

He deafens us
with the furious hymns
of his candles.

ASSASSINATION

an abrupt arm raised
the lapel which leaps from the revolver
the crunch the gasp
the eyelashes in the gravel

beyond where the police
bend into a ring of light
the celebrated statue is spread
on the street like a stain
its hand rolling away to the gutter
the snapshot in its pants pocket
growing larger than a tree

a red flower blooms from its mouth
a clamshell goes on opening and closing
secondhands spilling from it
like jackstraws the sirens
are eaten by their echoes
the stub of blood is left
to burn itself out on the sidewalk

SCATTERING FLOWERS

It is our best and prayerful judgment that
they (air attacks) are a necessary part of the
surest road to peace.

— Lyndon B. Johnson

There is a dark tolling in the air,
an unbearable needle in the vein,
the horizon flaked with feathers of rust.
From the caves of drugged flowers
fireflies rise through the night:
they bear the sweet gospel of napalm.

Democracies of flame are declared
in the villages, the rice-fields
seethe with blistered reeds.
Children stand somnolent on their crutches.
Freedom, a dancing girl,
lifts her petticoats of gasoline,
and on the hot sands of the deserted beach
a wild horse struggles, choking
in the noose of diplomacy.

Now in the cane chairs the old men
who listen for the bitter wind
of bullets, spread on their thighs
maps, portfolios, legends of hair,
and photographs of dark Asian youths
who are already dissolving into broken water.

THE DAY THE WAR WAS OVER

the edible mandolin
disappeared into
the gold standard
autistic tongues
soared among
the cumulus clouds
muttering
with relief
the machine-guns
fell through a hole
in my pants pocket
my spine grew
into a tower
and sent out
leaves
I put my dry lips
to the drowned
magnet
and offered it
artificial respiration
everyone else
got drunk and sent
their boots
to sea

THE HOUR OF THE WOLF

— after Ingmar Bergman

Take me to Point Lobos, you said;
in that other life I looked south,
unfulfilled, to cypresses. There
on the beach I'd thought to see

what lay in wait at its rim; the smiling
deceptive boy, that succubus, fishing
from the rocks yet ready to leap
on my shoulders and bear me down

to the dark devouring surf. Take me
to Point

Lobos, you said, I've lived
too long at the wolf's hour and would
by its weight be borne down

or set free. Later, you laughed and made
the long stair down on our own —
but I marvelled at every step how close
those wolves those waves bore near.

TRAINING THE INDUSTRIAL MOUSTACHE

you open the valise you step out
you arrange yourself in orderly rows
brushing the hair on the left side
to the left and on the right side
to the right the knives and forks
are spread on the table the battle
is about to begin the Chateau Laffitte
uncorks itself the napkins take flight
you comb the white hair growing from
your knee to the right you comb
the green hair to the left you manicure
your elbows you wipe the wax
from the candlesticks the clock strikes
and strikes again you read the New
York Times for 1½ minutes everything
is ready at last you open the valise and

step in

HOW TO SURVIVE IN THE CITY OF
DREADFUL NIGHT

take care not to step in the boiling milk
which flows down the esplanade
look out for seaweed on the escalator
and the wind blowing on the plumed bone

embroider the high-rise with snowflakes
encourage each crystal you meet
keep away from elaborate peptalks
by the man with the french-fried teeth

don't fraternize with the hiccup
or the belch with the two-toned shoes
don't live too long with emery-cloth
never wear gloves in a storm

autonomous hands will present you
with keys and a drive-away car
say no to the man at the toll-gate
get away fast and as far as you can

A DAY OF ALARMS & OLD CLOUDS

I follow the clogged stream,
its willows bare of catkins.
Beyond the quarry the last
cliffs, surf, a frontier of fish.
A buzzard in the sea-wind,
the distant rocks wrapped
in gauze, the torn clouds black
with the weight of new rain.

Sudden cataracts of light
on the broken pasture.

The stream disappears in the dunes.
A voice comes from the wet earth
reciting litanies of sawdust,
of lost leaves and of mortality.

THE YEARS

one day drives out another the red sun
a hammer the cold stars the heads
of breathing nails

the seed is slaughtered the meadows
turn black from old fires
the singing birds nailed up on rustic crosses
a warning to travellers

the weeks are eaten by swarms of ants
the months open their vegetative maws

malice grows fat simplicity
leans on its snow-shovel hopeless
against each day's tide of paper

the day which presents us with its gifts
of calluses and magnetic warts

I close my eyes and see the manes of lions
entangled in the exhaustpipes
of glittering Porsches

every hour a suicide
buried unshriven in its mailslot

I awake in the night my windows open
the shadows of mountains afloat in the air
dripping amethyst and sapphire
from the great field of gravestones
gleaming in the Milky Way

SEEKING FORGIVENESS

I kneel before the Idol
swathed in its bloody bandages

I discover mechanical palaces
atriums where Aphrodite

blesses the slot machines
over and over

the loud-speakers
play symphonic variations

I swim in the turbid sea
salmon leaping in my bloodstream

photos flash off and on
inside my retina: snapshots

of old loves decayed villas
on the pink sand, beaches

strewn with palm-leaf and
whitened bone gifts of

my imagination's
relentless surf.

FINAL DAYS

At the door to
the vault a
bulldog with a
plastic whip in
its teeth

in the micro
scope slides of
dead flies

The gen -
erations
pass

ultimately
even internal
combustion
must disappear
in the Gulf of
Geology.

Maya a la Playa, 2001

5.

"Writing poetry, to me, is always a question of the present moment, so it's where I am right now that interests me. I'm always concerned with what I'm going to write next. When I go back to some of my poetry, I find it evocative. It is evocative not only of states of mind which existed when I wrote it, but it is evocative of something more than that. It becomes a new experience, too, even to the person who's written it.

Poetry, for the most part, is an act of joy for me. It is moment after moment after moment in which the poet creates something and alters reality in the course of it, which is the beauty of poetry even though nobody recognizes it. To me, the poetic moment is everything, and the historical process— I couldn't care less. When they come to evaluate the historical process and what's going on in this country, I'll be long dead. But no one will take away from me the moments of poetic creation and reshaping the world. "

— from interview with George Hitchcock
in *Durak,* No. 1

DAYS IN THE CITY

Faces on the jetty:
voyagers:
members of bridge clubs,
collectors of arthritis.

> Mr. Ravazzini
> studies the *boccie* court,
> runs, spins, lets go.

The unintellectual gulls
pursue each other
over the dirty sand.

Fog builds its nest
in the eucalyptus trees.
Old people at the church
of The Holy Name
sit waiting for hope
to emerge from its ship
of bells.

Crab-pots lowered
on glistening cords
into the choppy water.

> Voyagers:
>
> runs, spins, lets go.

DAYLIGHT SAVING

throw away the traffic charts say
goodbye to the queen of podiums she
won't miss you her microphone
has leukemia it leaks neckties
cancel that date with the ortho-
dontist forget the chalk talk and
the air-conditioned interview

listen to the wind admonish
the leaves its daughters
cultivate the combustible
lark in the sky the cicada
with its brash fiddle the blue
ventriloquist in the pinetree

your absence won't really
be noticed the directors
are on their third martini
so set your clock back
a dozen years and
take a deep breath

LANDSCAPE AFTER MAX ERNST

Verdigris &
blossoming
mould
spangled fish
rising like
demons through
murky water

wan bathers
with the grace
of corrupted
idols
on the ashen
beach:
rain:
flakes of rust
falling
in sudden
bouquets:

long rows
of deliquescent
deckchairs.

WITNESS

to all wharves I have known
gangways hatchcovers in pools
of oil coils of fanged
cables pallets cargo-booms
burlap sacks their swollen feet
carried on forkprong trucks

steel plates marked with my
blood hooks grapples fingers
of chain discarded burning now
in fires of rust birds screeching
keyholes of fog stern-voiced

winches the orchards of rivets
timeclocks of hemp and rice
with worn knuckles of salt
and the face of endless Mondays

and under the planks oilslick
a surge of sea-water - you!
mother of bottles bloated puffers
gloves without fingers lost skiffs
and the spent skin of oranges!

LEASE EXPIRED MUST SELL

Cement flowers
        in the park
        ingstrips meters
        like shrubs Equi

table Life gives
        birth to
        a spawn of awn
        ings striped clipped

on aluminum
        bones Printed
        smiles scotch
        taped to glass per

sistent hemorrhages
        in the stucco His
        tory a record of art

ifacts chrome horns
        aprons elastic
        undies lime and
        silicon Every

THING MUST GO

TWO POEMS FOR TRAVELERS

LAST CALL

Hurry up hurryup friends
we've got to get a move on
a trainload of open mouths
is waiting for us
at Rockabye station

Move along movealong please
I've come to herald the
chromatic revolution I've
come to announce the age
of implosion we mustn't
be late for the barricades

No time notimeleft
for marzipan no time
for badminton or RSVP's
someone just tossed a brick
through the plateglass window
and the naked mannequins
have all come down with AIDS

So pack your comb and some
dripdries don't forget
your Rolex we've
got to be there on the dot
when the camellia leaps

from the brakeman's pocket
and begins its final dance

JUST KEEP GOING

Where to now?
Look at the map.
It's smudged.
It always was.
I left my glasses.
Where?
At the motel.
Well, we can't go back.
Why not?
We can't, that's all.
Which way then?
Adelante!
That's the only way?
That's the only way.
Despite—?
Despite it all.
Despite the rancid air the snot the dead
fuchsias the crutches the burning navels
and the tired hats of filthy snow?
In spite of everything.
All right, take up your pack.
I've got it.
Adelante?
Adelante.

QUETZALAN

Where the cliffs drop toward Vera Cruz
I sat on the steps beneath a stained sky
waiting for the magic light to come back.

A parakeet squawked in the *posada* window
and an Indian woman by the *farmacia*
conjured up brooks of yarn. Yet still

I was cursed with the eight shadows
of porphyry: nothing came right.
I looked at the tapestry and saw there

not life but the frozen huntsman
and a *trompe l'oeil* on the kitchen door:
the pheasant painted larger than itself.

So the myths stood still, the liquid
fell in my glass, time ran out. Over
the spires of Saint Xavier the Blessed

clouds spread their sooty wings;
the parrot squawked, the awnings flapped
in a language I'd never comprehend.

GOING BACK THERE

I said goodbye to the clock's brass teeth
goodbye to the clown cap of columbine

pressed between *sec* and *sembler*
in the foxed Larousse   someone

has left a sigh in the room
now the window won't open

I came up here wearing sleeves of mist
I wanted to hear the bees roar again

to look for the missing star
in the bare twigs of the buckeye

the winter sun is pale a soft lace
of fennel sprouts from the wet earth

the wound is gone I've thrown
away even its reflection

someone's dream rustles the curtains
then falls like a gull's shadow

mottling the intricate sea of the rug

ONLY WHAT IS THERE IS THERE

the mirror on the beach
the beach in the mirror
the sandpiper runs up and down
crocheting the edges of the mirror
which holds the beach and the piper
while the sea is busy
unravelling the sand
as its breakers flow in and out
of the mirror which lies prostrate
on the merely reflected beach

The Cellist, 1999

6.

"To me, poetry is music. I'm writing in rhythms. Sometimes I'm writing in lines—it's hard to generalize. But nearly always, the most important thing for me in writing a poem is to get some musical sense before I start to write. Some sense of the rhythm. Not the content. Not even the words. The rhythm of a particular line will appeal to me first. Then I will repeat that rhythm in variations and then I will start writing down—while thinking that rhythm, while feeling that rhythm—all sorts of nonsense. Anything that comes to my head. Then, when I've sufficiently covered or disfigured a page with these chicken tracks, the problem is to find the center of it—what it revolves around. The problem is to define what you now have so that it is communicable to someone else, but not overdefine it—what you have then is a prose statement. If you approach the conscious too closely, then it's no longer a poem. On the other hand, if you don't approach the conscious—if you don't touch the shores of the conscious some place or another—then it is probably not a communicable poem."

— from interview with George Hitchcock
  in *Durak*, No. 1

HOME TOWN

My uncle sets me adrift
in a box on a pine plank.

I voyage to the land
of the eagles where I
marry and grow firm.

In my suit of feathers
I fly to the Township
of Complacency
where my uncle fishes.
I seize him by the hair.
Vengeamce. I say.
Aieee! my uncle cries.
His wife runs from the house,
grabs him by the ankle.

With my new wings
I pull them both aloft.
My cousin comes from
the schoolhouse, catches
the hem of her mother's dress.
Vengeance, I say.
Come down, she answers.

One by one all the people
of that wretched town
run out of their houses.

They grab each other
by ankles, knees, trousers,
shawls, dresses, fish-lines,
toes and members.

Their weight is nothing
against the strength
of my eagle's wings.
I carry them, a great chain,
out over the Bay
of Forgetfulness
and let go.

(after a Tlingit Indian myth)

SILENCE PLEASE

the alphabet sings
in a drop of blood

the power of verbs
is just a pious memory

take up the mountains
in hands of lace they're

a bargain no one
will give you as much

for your poems don't
say a word just let

the leaves speak for
you the raindrops wag

their tails and the sad
beaches talk with their

fellow atheists the surf
there is the way to ill

ustrate our origins
not with ink and disquiet

but with an almost im
perceptible shiver

HAMMER, NAILS, SAW

a hammer goes to the river
looking for nails
the fish dart away they're
not illiterate those fish

a saw comes by on the back
of a swan singing:
we must learn to nail the water
we must learn to saw the air
we must learn to undress clouds
there are gods inside waiting
to get out

the bulrushes snicker
the smart fish hide in deep pools
they know a thing or two those fish
they've heard that talk before

this life isn't easy
says the hammer to the saw
I'm just doing the job I was hired to do
says the saw to the speechless river

the river with a rip down its back
not even nails can mend

THE LADDER

the ladder is largely illiterate
and until recent times practiced
parthenogenesis

the ladder does not wear pockets
or nurse its young

accustomed to heights its rungs
are often found
at great altitudes
commonly amidst the detritus
of downspouts or growing
in crevices at the summit
of mansards

the ladder is readily domesticated
but reverts on occasion
to predatory ways
promiscuously devouring
footsteps and birds' eggs

a flight of ladders
loping over the veldt with
awkward though leisurely paces
is a noteworthy sight

shy when alone
a pride of ladders is capable
of a show of bravery
particularly
when protecting its young

the ladder is often entangled
in awnings where it may
by the amateur
be mistaken for the lesser scaffold
the distinctive mottling
however
differs sharply

the throat of the ladder suffers
from parasitic growths but
its only known natural enemy is
the high voltage wire

contrary to tradition ladders
do not commonly
lead to heaven

CALCULUS

the theory of the knife is simple:
it exists to bring multiple fractions
to tangerines   it sings at its work
in the morning and lies down to rest
in velvet or wood at night
it does not often complain
it prefers flesh to cartilage
cartilage to bone and avoids
the ineluctable teeth of raindrops

RECORDS

Another
Russian
has returned
after 2,000,000
miles
in orbit.

Today I sat
motionless
for
28
minutes
while a
butterfly
folded its
trembling
wings
and rested
on my knee.

Also by George Hitchcock

Plays

Five Plays (Jazz/Papa Bach)
The Counterfeit Rose
The Discovery and Ascent of Kan-Chen-Chomo

Poetry

Poems & Prints
Tactics of Survival
The Rococo Eye
Ship of Bells
The Dolphin with a Revolver in its Teeth
Lessons in Alchemy
The Piano Beneath the Skin
Mirror on Horseback
Cloud Taxis
The Wounded Alphabet

Stories

Notes of the Siege Year
October at the Lighthouse

Novels

Another Shore
The Racquet

Anthologies

Losers Weepers: An anthology of Found Poems
Pioneers of Modern Poetry (with Robert Peters)